EARTHWAYS

EARTHWISE

For Phyllis Hunt, with thanks.

Oxford University Press, Great Clarendon Street, Oxford OX2 6DP

Oxford New York
Athens Auckland Bangkok Bogota Bombay
Buenos Aires Calcutta Cape Town Dar es Salaam Delhi
Florence Hong Kong Istanbul Karachi
Kuala Lumpur Madras Madrid Melbourne
Mexico City Nairobi Paris Singapore
Taipei Tokyo Toronto Warsaw

and associated companies in
Berlin Ibadan

Oxford is a trade mark of Oxford University Press

Copyright © Judith Nicholls 1993
First published 1993
Reprinted in paperback 1995
Reprinted in paperback with new cover 1997, 1998

ISBN 0 19 272248 4

The illustrations are by:

Claire Hemstock Chapter 1, pages 7, 8-9, 10, 11, 14, 15, 19;
Cathy Morley Chapter 2, pages 20-21, 22-23, 24-25, 28-29, 30-31;
Caroline Smith Chapter 3, pages 32-33, 34-35, 38-39, 40-41;
Helen Holroyd Chapter 4, pages 42, 43, 44, 45, 46-47, 48-49, 50, 52-53, 56, 57;
Alison Wisenfeld Chapter 5, pages 58, 59, 60, 61, 62, 63, 64, 65;
Rachel Ross Chapter 6, pages 66-67, 68-69, 70-71, 72, 74-75, 76-77;
Rosemary Woods Chapter 7, pages 78-79, 80-81, 82-83, 84-85, 88-89, 90-91; 92-93.

Sheila Moxley Cover illustration and title pages.

A CIP catalogue record for this book is available from the British Library

Printed in Hong Kong on acid-free paper

Set in 12 point Sabon.

EARTHWAYS

Poems on Conservation
Selected by Judith Nicholls

EARTHWISE

OXFORD UNIVERSITY PRESS
Oxford New York Toronto

CONTENTS

Tiny grass,
your steps are small . . .

Whale, I hear you calling . . .

Enjoy the earth gently

What on earth

are we doing . . . ?

What on Earth?

What on earth are we doing?
Once wood-pigeons flew,
and young badgers tunnelled
where oak and ash grew . . .

*Now the forest's a runway
and all that flies through
is a whining grey plane
where the pigeons once flew.*

Where on earth are we going?
At the end of the lane
once blackberries hung
in soft Autumn rain . . .

*Now the lane is a car-park,
and never again
will fruit fill our baskets
down in the lane.*

Why on earth are we crying?
Once morning dew shone
on hawthorn and primrose,
caught in the sun . . .

*Now the forest is carpeted
only with stone.
No primrose, no hawthorn;
the forest has gone.*

Judith Nicholls

General Winter

I stand in native woodland,
My gaze goes all around.
The muted shades of Autumn
Lie dark'ning on the ground.

But surely it's not Autumn,
We've just begun July.
The stark, bare, waving branches
Trace patterns on the sky.

Oh will the green of Springtime
Touch dying woods again?
For now is General Winter.
One season, Acid Rain.

Ian Larmont

Acid Rain

Acid rain
falls on the grass
falls on the grain
falls on the mountain
falls on the plain
falls on the flower
falls on the crane
falls on the lake
falls on the lane
falls on the flats
falls on the drain
falls on the tree
falls on the train
acid rain
acid rain
acid rain
acid rain

Charles Thomson

The Bird's Nest

I know a place, in the ivy on a tree,
Where a bird's nest is, and the eggs are three,
And the bird is brown, and the eggs are blue,
And the twigs are old, but the moss is new,
And I go quite near, though I think I should have heard
The sound of me watching, if I had been a bird.

John Drinkwater

Riddle

Within white seamless walls
I store my treasure,
A gold that nourishes.
Search as you will
You will find no opening in me.
Once shattered I'm not for mending.

John Cotton

Answer: An egg

They

they tapped and tapped on the shell
and the shell broke
and the yolk broke

cracked they said it's cracked

then they opened the cracked shell wide
  and cried

                    and cried

Mervyn Morris

I'm a Parrot

I'm a parrot
I live in a cage
I'm nearly always
in a vex-up rage

I used to fly
all light and free
in the luscious
green forest canopy

I'm a parrot
I live in a cage
I'm nearly always
in a vex-up rage

I miss the wind
against my wing
I miss the nut
and the fruit picking

I'm a parrot
I live in a cage
I'm nearly always
in a vex-up rage

I squawk I talk
I curse I swear
I repeat the things
I shouldn't hear

I'm a parrot
I live in a cage
I'm nearly always
in a vex-up rage

So don't come near me
or put out your hand
because I'll pick you
if I can

    pickyou
    pickyou
    if I can

I want to be free
CAN'T YOU UNDERSTAND

Grace Nichols

The Dodo

The Dodo used to walk around,
    And take the sun and air.
The sun yet warms his native ground —
    The Dodo is not there!

The voice which used to squawk and squeak
    Is now for ever dumb —
Yet may you see his bones and beak
    All in the Mu-se-um.

Hilaire Belloc

Stones

I like stones.
I like to touch
their shape and colour:
such, and such.
Lift one up
and you may find
tiny creatures
there confined
hidden safely
out of sight
in a small
and private night.

Stones are quiet,
stones are cold.
Some of them
are old — so old
that upon
their surface clings
a pattern of
the strangest things:
leaves, and fish,
and shells and seas
and birds from different
skies than these
when the Earth
had just begun.

Stones know more
than anyone.

Jean Kenward

The House That Jack Built

This is the house that Jack built.

This is the stone
that made the house that Jack built.

This is the rain
that fell on the stone
that made the house that Jack built.

These are the gases
that mixed with the rain
that fell on the stone
that made the house that Jack built.

These are the fumes
that carried the gases
that mixed with the rain
that fell on the stone
that made the house that Jack built.

These are the cars
that breathed out the fumes
that carried the gases
that mixed with the rain
that fell on the stone
that made the house that Jack built.

These are the men
who drove the cars
that breathed out the fumes
that carried the gases
that mixed with the rain
that fell on the stone
that made the house that Jack built.

This is Jack
who's one of the men
who drove the cars
that breathed out the fumes
that carried the gases
that mixed with the rain
that fell on the stone . . .

that *once* was the house that Jack built.

Judith Nicholls

Would You . . . ?

How would you like to see
earth's face shaved clean
of grass and tree?
Not me!

How would you like to hear
the sound of thrush
and robin disappear?
No fear!

How would you like to try
to live upon an earth
where forests die?
Not I!

Judith Nicholls

My Future

What will be
Left here for me
When I grow up?

Will there be
Pure air to breathe
Will the sea be clean?

Will tarmac
Cover all the fields
Will they still be green?

Milk from cows
Meat, veg and fruit
Will they be fit to eat?

Will sunlight hurt
Will fumes from cars
Clog up a crowded street?

Will blue whales sing
Will elephants
and rhinos still survive?

Will you have left
Us anything
Healthy and alive?

When I've grown up
And I'm in charge
What will it be worth

If you have used
The goodness up
And destroyed the Earth?

David Harmer

Everything's Got Its Place

Everything's got its place,
everything's got its place.

We all need
spiders
snakes
sand and slugs,

bananas
bears
bats and bugs.

Everything's got its place,
everything's got its place.

We all need
cabbages
crabs
cats and crows,

wolves
wallabies
worms and us!

Everything's got its place,
everything's got its place.

Ian McMillan and Martyn Wiley

19

Where apple trees

Where Apple Trees Once Stood . . .

Where apple trees once stood
there stands a dirty lorry.
What was an apple orchard
has now become a quarry.

Where grasses used to grow
(till munched on by a cow),
the dumper trucks roar round
and stacks of bricks stand now.

Where once a picnic ground
stretched by the river bank,
the asphalt car-park holds
the cars parked rank on rank.

Where now the farmer works
to gather in the hay,
the planners have decided
to build a motorway.

Charles Thomson

once stood . . . .

What is One?

One is the sun,
a rhino's horn;
a drop of dew,
a lizard's tongue.

One is the world,
a lonely whale;
an elephant's trunk,
a monkey's tail.

One is an acorn,
one is a moon;
one is a forest,
felled too soon.

Judith Nicholls

Surrounded by Noise!

I'm surrounded by noise,
LISTEN!

BEEP! BEEP! BEEP!
A car down on the street.
BOOGIE! BOOGIE! BOOGIE!
A disco beat.

THUMP! THUMP! THUMP!
A hammer next door.
THUD! THUD! THUD!
Brother jumping on the floor.

CLACKETY! CLACKETY! CLACKETY!
A train rattles by.
ROAR! ROAR! ROAR!
A plane climbs the sky.

DRILL! DRILL! DRILL!
A workman on the road.
NO! NO! NO!
Mum about to explode.

We're surrounded by noise,
Just . . . STOP!
Just . . . LISTEN!

Ian Souter

Machine Riddle

I am the breaker of bones
I am the fouler of air
    Watch out for me once
    then twice
    then again . . .
Beware, oh beware!

I am the beast of sight
I can find my prey anywhere
    I can see what's to come
    what is now
    what is past . . .
Beware, oh beware!

And at night by my beacon sight
I follow a trail to my lair
The gleaming spoor of
    blood-
      red
        eyes . . .
Beware, oh beware!

Mick Gowar

Answer: A car

23

There's a Dragon

There's a dragon in a motor car,
    a dragon, so it's said,
a dragon in a motor car
    that fills the air with lead.

There's a dragon in a chimney stack,
    a dragon, it's no joke,
a dragon in a chimney stack
    that fills the sky with smoke.

There's a dragon in the ocean waves,
    just watch its limbs uncoil,
a dragon in the ocean waves
    that drowns the birds in oil.

There's a dragon by the river bank
    who has an evil wish,
all day it drivels toxic saliva
    that kills off all the fish.

There's a dragon underneath the ground
    whose power will not pass,
it sweats out noxious chemicals
    that poison crops and grass.

There's a dragon in the power station,
    all year it quietly breathes,
there's a dragon in the power station
    that could fill whole towns with wreaths.

There's a dragon in the missile site,
    we watch it gently sleep,
there's a dragon in the missile site
    that could make the whole world weep.

There's a dragon in the heart of man,
    invisible as a rule,
there's a dragon in the heart of man,
    the most dangerous dragon of all.

Charles Thomson

Mummy, Oh Mummy

'Mummy, Oh Mummy, what's this pollution
That everyone's talking about?'
'Pollution's the mess that the country is in,
That we'd all be far better without.
It's factories belching their fumes in the air,
And the beaches all covered with tar,
Now throw all those sweet papers into the bushes
Before we get back in the car.'

'Mummy, Oh Mummy, who makes pollution,
And why don't they stop if it's bad?'
''Cos people like that just don't think about others,
They don't think at all, I might add.
They spray all the crops and they poison the flowers,
And wipe out the birds and the bees,
Now there's a good place we could dump that old mattress
Right out of sight in the trees.'

'Mummy, Oh Mummy, what's going to happen
If all the pollution goes on?'
'Well the world will end up like a second-hand junk-yard,
With all of its treasures quite gone.
The fields will be littered with plastics and tins,
The streams will be covered with foam,
Now throw those two pop bottles over the hedge,
Save us from carting them home.'

'But Mummy, Oh Mummy, if I throw the bottles,
Won't that be polluting the wood?'
'Nonsense! that isn't the same thing at all,
You just shut up and be good.
If you're going to start getting silly ideas
I'm taking you home right away,
'Cos pollution is something that other folk do,
We're just enjoying our day.'

Anon.

All Things Bright . . .

All things bright and beautiful
Will soon be dead and gone
All things wise and wonderful
Man soon will kill them all.

Matthew Baird (Age 10)

Christmas Eve

(for Daniel)

In a brilliant universe I know
there was a luminous sun and its system

and in the luminous system
there was a half-bright planet

and on the half-bright planet
there was a cloudy continent

and in the cloudy continent
there was a sunless country

and in the sunless country
there was an obscure town

and in the obscure town
there was an unlit street

and in the unlit street
there was a dark house

and in the dark house
there was a child

with an idea
about a bright house

and a brilliant universe
I know.

Fred Sedgwick

From My Window

Lights of the power station
at night
over the water
like runny paint on a paper.

It's beautiful.

Flames from the chemical works
at night
against the sky
like a dragon's breath.

It's beautiful.

Steam from the cooling towers
at night
covering the Moon
like a white scarf.

It's beautiful.

I live near the power station.
I live near the chemical works.
I live near the cooling towers.
At night
it hurts to breathe.

It's ugly.

Martyn Wiley and Ian McMillan

Song of the Sky Loom

O our Mother the Earth, O our Father the Sky,
Your children are we, and with tired backs
We bring you the gifts you love.
Then weave for us a garment of brightness;
May the warp be the white light of morning,
May the weft be the red light of evening,
May the fringes be the falling rain,
May the border be the standing rainbow.
Thus weave for us a garment of brightness,
That we may walk fittingly where grass is green,
O our Mother the Earth, O our Father the Sky.

Tewa (North American Indian)

I Spy on the Road

RED METAL ROAD SIGN,
CONCRETE BRIDGE, BUILDING SITES,
ROWS OF LORRIES, CARS, COACHES,
STOP, GO, TRAFFIC LIGHTS,

ROUNDABOUT, FACTORIES,
NO ENTRY, SHOPPING STORES,
TRAFFIC WARDENS, CAR PARK,
OFFICE BLOCK (20 FLOORS).

Mummy, what's that?
Over there — can you see?
That thing coloured green.
That, my dear, is a tree.

Charles Thomson

Acorn Haiku

Just a green olive
In its own little egg-cup:
It can feed the sky.

Kit Wright

Be still, my heart,

these great trees are prayers . . .
Rabindranath Tagore

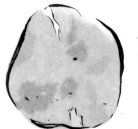

Words

In woods are words.
You hear them all,
Winsome, witless or wise,
When the birds call.

In woods are words.
If your ears wake
You hear them, quiet and clear,
When the leaves shake.

In woods are words.
You hear them all
Blown by the wet wind
When raindrops fall.

In woods are words
Kind or unkind;
Birds, leaves and hushing rain
Bring them to mind.

James Reeves

Fun fun fungi

Shhh! There is a secret in the woods
at autumn time
when leaves drip from the trees
and beads of dew hang like jewels
from spiders' webs
there is a secret in the woods
when cold winds
come whispering
fun fun fungi
from damp dark places
they rise and grow
toadstools
mushrooms
and fungi which cling and creep
along fallen logs
and in the hollows of trees
the fun fun fungi
of fairy rings

Robert Fisher

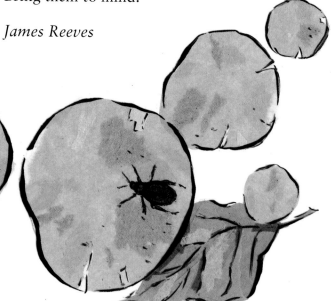

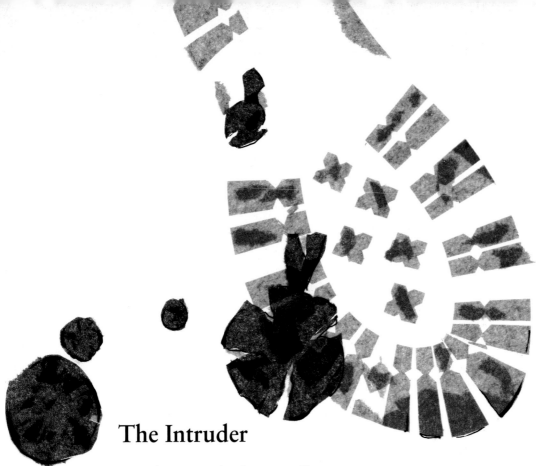

The Intruder

Two-boots in the forest walks,
Pushing through the bracken stalks.

Vanishing like a puff of smoke,
Nimbletail flies up the oak.

Longears helter-skelter shoots
Into his house among the roots.

At work upon the highest bark,
Tapperbill knocks off to hark.

Painted-wings through sun and shade
Flounces off along the glade.

Not a creature lingers by,
When clumping Two-boots comes to pry.

James Reeves

Trees

Trees are the kindest things I know,
They do no harm, they simply grow

And spread a shade for sleepy cows,
And gather birds among their boughs.

They give us fruit in leaves above,
And wood to make our houses of,

And leaves to burn on Hallowe'en
And in the Spring new buds of green.

They are the first when day's begun
To touch the beams of morning sun,

They are the last to hold the light
When evening changes into night,

And when a moon floats on the sky
They hum a drowsy lullaby

Of sleepy children long ago . . .
Trees are the kindest things I know.

Harry Behn

Ten Tall Oaktrees

Ten tall oaktrees
Standing in a line,
'Warships,' cried King Henry,
Then there were nine.

Nine tall oaktrees
Growing strong and straight,
'Charcoal,' breathed the furnace,
Then there were eight.

Eight tall oaktrees
Reaching towards heaven,
'Sizzle,' spoke the lightning,
Then there were seven.

Seven tall oaktrees,
Branches, leaves and sticks,
'Firewood,' smiled the merchant,
Then there were six.

Six tall oaktrees
Glad to be alive,
'Barrels,' boomed the brewery,
Then there were five.

Five tall oaktrees,
Suddenly a roar,
'Gangway,' screamed the west wind,
Then there were four.

Four tall oaktrees
Sighing like the sea,
'Floorboards,' beamed the builder,
Then there were three.

Three tall oaktrees
Groaning as trees do,
'Unsafe,' claimed the council,
Then there were two.

Two tall oaktrees
Spreading in the sun,
'Progress,' snarled the by-pass,
Then there was one.

One tall oaktree
Wishing it could run,
'Nuisance,' grumped the farmer,
Then there were none.

No tall oaktrees,
Search the fields in vain,
Only empty skylines
And the cold grey rain.

Richard Edwards

Red Alert

Flame-tail!
Crackerjack!
Racing to the top and back!
Slim, trim,
Full of vim,
Chasing out along a limb!
Dash, dart,
Stop and start;
Dark spark
Against the bark;
Lick of red
Overhead;
Live wire
Leaping higher;
FOREST FIRE!

Gina Wilson

Coal

Black diamonds,
Hard earned.
Flames licking,
Soon burned.

Wendy Larmont

Firelight

Last night
as flames curled round my coal
I thought I saw
a million years ago
a forest fall.

Judith Nicholls

Our Tree

It takes so long for a tree to grow
So many years of pushing the sky.

Long branches stretch their arms
Reach out with their wooden fingers.

Years drift by, fall like leaves
From green to yellow then back to green.

Since my Grandad was a boy
And then before his father's father

There's been an elm outside our school
Its shadow long across our playground.

Today three men ripped it down.
Chopped it up. It took ten minutes.

David Harmer

from **Forest**

The forest stretches for miles,
a place where labourers
poached rabbit for the pot,
where deer roamed free.
An ancient place, root and tree
firmly established,
majestic oaks spreading
into an eternity of time.

Still those oaks, now shedding
tough brown leaves, are here.
The forest floor rustles
with the dry sound of leaf
upon leaf of history.
Oak and birch set new seed,
regenerate themselves,
and slender saplings rise.

The forest is evolving, ever-
changing, yet the same.
Belonging to itself, never
planted, never tame.
Let this wish be granted:
that the forest will remain.

Ann Bonner

Hurt no living thing...

Hurt No Living Thing

Hurt no living thing,
Ladybird nor butterfly,
Nor moth with dusty wing,
Nor cricket chirping cheerily,
Nor grasshopper, so light of leap,
Nor dancing gnat,
Nor beetle fat,
Nor harmless worms that creep.

Christina Rossetti

Percy Pot-Shot

Percy Pot-Shot went out hunting,
Percy Pot-Shot and his gun,
Percy Pot-Shot, such a hot shot,
Shot a sparrow, said 'What fun!'

Percy Pot-Shot shot a blackbird,
Shot a lapwing, shot a duck,
Shot a swan as it rose flapping,
Shot an eagle, said 'What luck!'

Percy Pot-Shot shot a rabbit,
Shot a leaping gold-eyed hare,
Shot a tiger that lay sleeping,
Shot a rhino, shot a bear.

Percy Pot-Shot, trigger happy,
Shot a fountain, shot a tree,
Shot a river, shot a mountain,
Shot some rainclouds, shot the sea.

Percy Pot-Shot went on hunting,
Percy Pot-Shot and his gun,
Not a lot that he had not shot,
Shot the moon down, shot the sun.

Percy Pot-Shot stood in darkness,
No bird fluttered, no beast stirred,
Percy Pot-Shot knelt and muttered
'God forgive me.' No one heard.

Richard Edwards

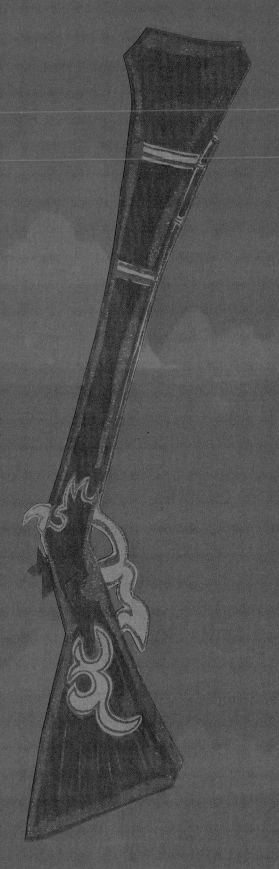

The Bear

Chained to his pole, the dancing bear
Waltzes across the village square.

His keeper skips along the middle
Scraping a tune on an old cracked fiddle.

With leather boots and scarlet shirt
He leads the creature through the dirt.

The great beast lumbers round and round
While coins are flung upon the ground.

Pity the clumsy dancing bear
Who used to breathe the forest air.

Gerard Benson

The Elephant Dance

The music plays
They lumber in
Jennet
Jelopher
And Trumbokin,
The trumpet brays
And Jennet sways
In Mister Mazurka's Circus.

Jelopher clumsily pirouettes
Twirls her grey bulk slowly round
Then down she sets
Upon the ground
The ballerina from her back
In Mister Mazurka's Circus.

Trumbokin polkas like a clown
Hops a step then tumbles down
Rolls over on his massive back
In Mister Mazurka's Circus.

But when night comes
They softly dream
Jennet
Jelopher
And Trumbokin,
Jennet of the Southern Star,
Jelopher of India,
Trumbokin of the dark green heat;
All of them sweetly, sweet-
ly dream — and travel far
From Mister Mazurka's Circus.

Gerard Benson

Wolf

Mine is the howl
that chills the spine
in the forest gloom;
mine is the whine.

Mine is the nose
that breathes in fear
when danger's close;
mine is the ear.

Mine is the fur
the huntsmen trade;
mine is the fur,
I am afraid.

Judith Nicholls

Guard Wolf

My coat is thick,
my teeth are strong.
The snow lies deep,
the winter's long.

I stand on guard
here in the cold.
The pack's asleep.
Some grow old.
In fairy tales
I roamed the wood,
the bad wolf in
Red Riding Hood.
I live by hunting.
Men hunt me.
When guns spit fire
I run. I flee.

My coat is thick,
my teeth are strong.
The snow lies deep,
the winter's long.

Wes Magee

Do You Know the Fox?

Do you know the fox with her coat so red?
She was born in a box, on a farm she was bred.
With her tail drooping down and a price on her head,
She is sad as a bird in a cage is —
Sad as a bird in a cage.

Do you know the trader? He puts profit first,
And the pockets of his coat hold a fat money purse
That he filled to the brim selling foxes' furs.
He is greedy as a desert for a rainstorm —
Greedy as a desert for the rain.

Do you know the lady with her coat so rare?
It was lined with sorrow and stitched with care.
Her beauty is as deep as the skins that she wears
And her heart is as cold as a stone is —
Her heart is as cold as a stone.

Do you know the fox with her coat so red?
With her white-tipped tail and her long-muzzled head,
The heather is her cover and the earth is her bed.
She is free as a breeze in the willows —
Free as a breeze in the tree.

Sandra Kerr

Riddle

Snow-motion, lumbering
Avalanche of fur,
From my wide glass kingdom
They brought me here

To your narrow world
Where the sky is grey
And white clouds are baffled
By each gloomy day.

John Mole

Answer: A polar bear

Bamboozled!

A polar bear just loves an icy landscape,
The eagle likes a mountain with a view;
A whale demands an oceanful of water . . .
All *I* want is a thicket of BAMBOO!

The magpie gathers sticks and straw for nesting,
For a woodlouse some rotting bark will do;
The rabbit digs her home beneath the forest . . .
For *mine* I just need old stalks of BAMBOO!

Some tasty mouse is buzzard's choice for dinner,
A field of grass is what a cow will chew;
Koalas can't resist their eucalyptus . . .
All *I* need is a bunch of ripe BAMBOO!

Please !

Judith Nicholls

Rhino on the Run

Sunrise over the Serengeti,
Creatures stir and begin their day.
One appears and the trees all tremble,
It's a young rhinoceros out to play!

> There's a one-ton, two-horned giant in the sun;
> It's a three-toed, four-legged rhino on the run.
> For he's all too rare, so do take care
> To shoot him with a camera and never with a gun.

Feeding time in the broad savannah,
White rhinoceros wander free;
Roll in dusty bath, feast on tender grass,
Snooze at peace in shade of tree.

> There's a one-ton, two-horned . . .

Sunset over the Serengeti,
To the water the thirsty creep.
White rhinoceros take your fill
And wander off to cover, then go to sleep.

> There's a one-ton, two-horned . . .

Children of Elland Church of England Junior School

from Snail Appeal

The snail said, 'Shall
I still
Be a snail
Safe and small
In my shell
When another
Summer's
Gone?'

Elma Mitchell

The Weeper

All alone, alone I dwell,
Captive within my bony shell,
A hermit in a hermit's cell.

I have no feet, I cannot walk;
I have no tongue, I cannot talk;
But eyes I have, each on a stalk —

Their dazzling drops of sorrow fall
In glints of silver over all,
As, silken, beneath the moon, I crawl.

Across the grass at dawn you see,
Shimmering, my tearful tracery;
No other creature weeps like me!

Gina Wilson

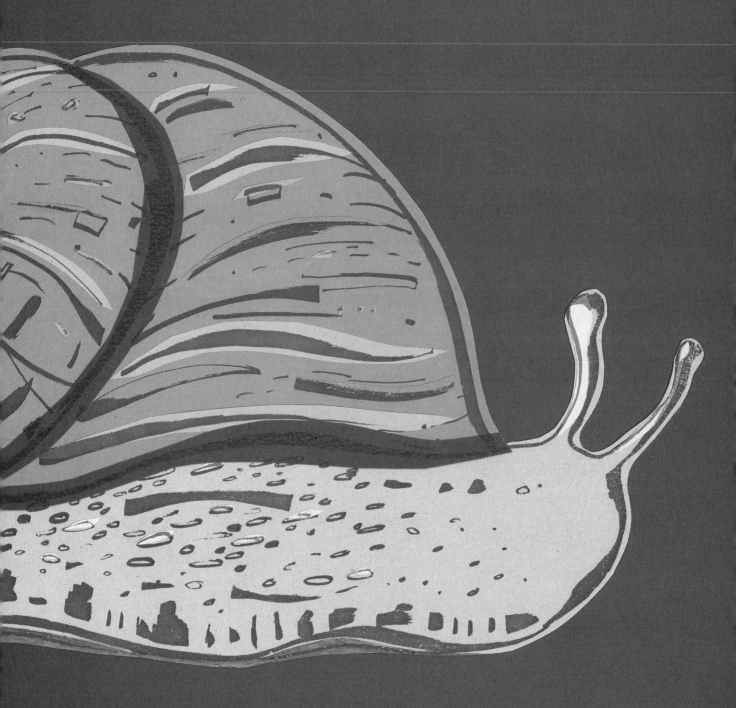

I Know an Old Lady

I know an old lady who killed all the flies,
I don't know why she killed all the flies;
Perhaps she'll die.

I know an old lady who killed all the spiders,
That wriggled and jiggled and tickled beside her.
She killed all the spiders that ate all the flies,
I don't know why she killed all the flies;
Perhaps she'll die.

I know an old lady who killed all the trees,
What a wheeze!
She killed all the trees.
She killed all the trees,
As well as the spiders,
That wriggled and jiggled and tickled beside her.
She killed all the spiders that ate all the flies,
I don't know why she killed all the flies;
Perhaps she'll die.

I know an old lady who killed all the fishes,
Tasty dishes!
She killed all those fishes.
She killed all the fishes as well as the trees,
She killed all the trees as well as the spiders,
That wriggled and jiggled and tickled beside her.
She killed all the spiders that ate all the flies,
I don't know why she killed all the flies;
Perhaps she'll die.

I know an old lady who killed all the grass,
To build a by-pass she killed all the grass.
She killed all the grass as well as the fishes,
She killed all the fishes as well as the trees,
She killed all the trees as well as the spiders,
That wriggled and jiggled and tickled beside her.
She killed all the spiders that ate all the flies,
I don't know why she killed all the flies;
Perhaps she'll die.

I know an old lady who polluted the air,
She didn't care!
She polluted the air —
Sh-e-e-'s no longer THERE.

Rose Reeder

Giants

How would *you* like it —
Supposing that *you* were a snail,
And your eyes grew out on threads,
Gentle, and small, and frail —
If an enormous creature,
Reaching almost up to the distant skies,
Leaned down, and with his great finger touched
your eyes
Just for the fun
Of seeing you snatch them suddenly in
And cower, quivering, back
Into your pitiful shell, so brittle and thin?
Would you think it was fun then?
Would you think it was fun?

And how would *you* like it,
Supposing you were a frog,
An emerald scrap with a pale, trembling throat
In a cool and shadowed bog,
If a tremendous monster,
Tall, tall, so that his head seemed lost in mist,
Leaned over, and clutched you up in his great fist
Just for the joy
Of watching you jump, scramble, tumble, fall,
In graceless, shivering dread,
Back into the trampled reeds that were grown so
tall?
Would you think it a joy then?
Would you think it a joy?

Lydia Pender

Hummingbird

Cried a scientist watching this creature dart by,
'Why, its wings are too small for it! How dare it fly?'

So he figured and figured and finally found
That it just couldn't possibly get off the ground,

And they made him Professor. But still, hummingbird
Kept on flying to flowerbeds. It hadn't heard.

X. J. Kennedy

Grasslands

The world tilts and I with it.
The wind blows and I bend.
Frail grass with tenuous roots,
I have my seasons and winter is long.

Vulnerable creatures scurry to my shelter.
Timid flowers bloom within my lee.
Beneath the surface, unseen,
Those delicate roots struggle to hold on.

Catherine Benson

Tiny grass,

your steps are small,

from **Stray Birds**

'We, the rustling leaves, have a voice that answers the storms, but who are you, so silent?'
'I am a mere flower.'

Rabindranath Tagore

but you possess the earth under your tread...

Rabindranath Tagore

Wild Flower

Our uncut lawn to me alone brings joy,
With shaggy dandelion suns, grass bound;
To me they are not weeds, do not annoy,
Each ragged clump of leaves with light seems crowned.
I cannot understand my father's haste
To week-end mow and sever every head;
Though pleasing him, it leaves a barren waste,
A bare expanse of green, where once was spread
An emerald carpet buttoned down with gold.
So it looks now, with here and there a cloud
Of softest grey as tawny heads grow old.
Unseen I pluck each clock and laugh aloud.
I know, of course, they do not tell the hour,
But breath-blown seeds will fall, take root . . . and flower!

Catherine Benson

Dandelion

Nobody winds the dandelion,
nobody oils his clock,
nobody counts his timely beat
tick . . . tick . . . tock.

Nobody sets the right alarm,
nobody holds his key,
nobody tells him what to do —
where to be.

Nobody fixes every seed
so, in a perfect ball,
each in his individual place —
nobody bids them fall . . .

Only a wind, a bit of a breeze,
only a wandering whim
blows him this or the other way —
roots and anchors him.

Jean Kenward

What is a Weed?

A bramble,
sweet with blackberries?
A wild rose,
sharp with thorns?
A nettle,
hung with butterflies?
A daisy,
starring lawns?

A dandelion,
lighting May?
A clover,
tipped with bees?
An ivy,
creeping round a shed?
Are *these*
really *weeds*?

Judith Nicholls

Afternoon on a Hill

I will be the gladdest thing
    Under the sun!
I will touch a hundred flowers
    And not pick one.

I will look at cliffs and clouds
    With quiet eyes,
Watch the wind bow down the grass,
    And the grass rise.

And when lights begin to show
    Up from the town,
I will mark which must be mine,
    And then start down!

Edna St. Vincent Millay

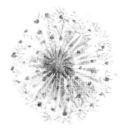

Seeds

I filled a tray with seeds —
French Marigold (from Mexico) —
To start them off, away from weeds.

I placed the tray in a dark room,
The curtain drawn (or so I thought).
I felt the seeds would feel at home.

French Marigold, known as Tiger Eyes:
I thought about the orange flower
And left the seeds alone for days.

Something must have moved one night:
The curtain wasn't closed at all,
Green shoots were leaning to the light.

Alan Bold

Planting

Bumpy, lumpy,
crisp and crunchy,
lying on the loam —
buy some bulbs
and plant them quickly
when you get them home.

Bumpy, lumpy,
crisp and crunchy,
tuck them underground . . .
What a welcome
they will bring you
when the Spring comes round!

Bumpy, lumpy,
crisp and crunchy,
suddenly you'll get
pink and purple,
orange, yellow,
crimson, violet!

Jean Kenward

Nicely, Nicely

Nicely, nicely, nicely, away in the east,
the rain clouds care for the little corn plants
as a mother cares for her baby.

Zuni Corn Ceremony

Whale
I hear you calling

Whalesong

I am
ocean voyager,
sky-leaper,
maker of waves;
I harm no man.

I know
only the slow tune
of turning tide,
the heave and sigh
of full seas meeting land
at dusk and dawn,
the sad whale song.
I harm no man.

Judith Nicholls

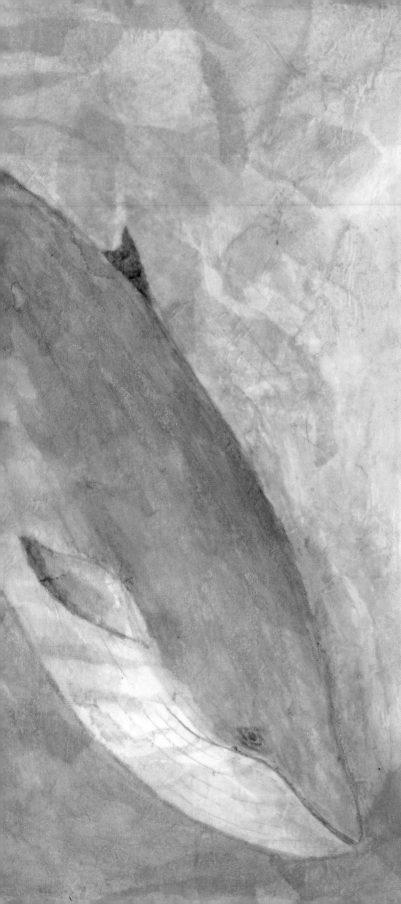

The Song of the Whale

Heaving mountain in the sea,
Whale, I heard you
Grieving.

Great whale, crying for your life,
Crying for your kind, I knew
How we would use
Your dying:

Lipstick for our painted faces,
Polish for our shoes.

Tumbling mountain in the sea,
Whale, I heard you
Calling.

Bird-high notes, keening,
Soaring:
At their edge a tiny drum
Like a heartbeat.

We would make you
Dumb.

In the forest of the sea,
Whale, I heard you
Singing.

Singing to your kind.
We'll never let you be.
Instead of life we choose

Lipstick for our painted faces,
Polish for our shoes.

Kit Wright

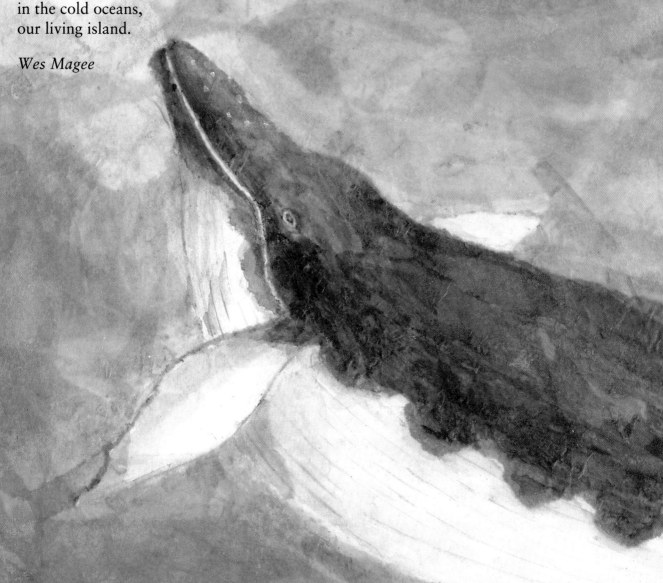

Humpback Whale

Our living island,
your sad song echoes
beneath the icebergs.

Survive and swim free
in the cold oceans,
our living island.

Wes Magee

Whale Haiku

our tears flood the sea
falling on troubled waters
numbers dwindling

Martin Cook (Age 11)

Whale

In this room, and the next, and the next,
you will see a whale; huge creatures once found
in all oceans of the world,
criss-crossing the waters,
sending the signals we failed to hear.
Till whales all but disappeared,
and then it was far too late.

We chased this one for several days,
repaired the damage the harpoon made,
and now this whale is as good as new.
This was the one they called *Big Blue*.

Brian Moses

The Whale

The whale, the whale,
The citizen of the sea,
He has the right to live
And so does she.
In the ocean, in the wild,
She moves peaceful with her child,
Till the harpoon wounds her young,
And she hovers to protect it,
And she's done.

The whale, the whale,
The citizen of the sea,
He sings his sonic song
And so does she.
He finds his mating ground
Till the whaler tracks him down,
Every quarter hour, they say,
One great whale is done away,
Done away.

The humpback and the blue,
The bowhead and the right,
Every quarter hour
Day and night.
Ocean creatures large and small,
There was room enough for all,
Till there came the rule of man,
Now the gentle whale is dogmeat
In the can.

The whale, the whale,
Four millions used to be
Their rightful population
In the sea.
Few thousands now remain
And we harry them again,
As the whale goes, and the dolphin,
And the ocean, and the forest,
So will we.

Malvina Reynolds

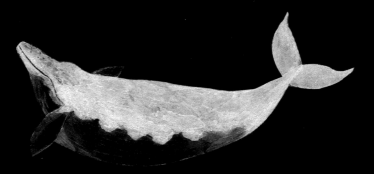

Seal-Song

In a faintly blue tinged crystal sea
a seal has turned to look at me,
deep black eyes and body long,
it sings its own seal-song.

'Oh keep my waters deep and fresh
and let there be many fish,
let all my friends swim next to me
this is a seal's true wish.

And keep the blackness from the waves
and poison from the air,
let gulls and cormorants dive within
our waters, while we're there.

Let our friends, who live on land,
know the sea is deep and long,
and there is room for everyone
who can hear my own seal-song.'

In a faintly blue tinged crystal sea
a seal has turned to look at me,
deep black eyes and body long,
it sings its own seal-song.

Robin Mellor

Where Have the Seals Gone?

Where have the seals gone? Where are the whales
That once used our waters before there were sails?
Where are the emus that once used to roam
The fields and the forests we've turned into home?

    They've all gone away as the sun turns to rain.
    I live here and wonder will they ever
    Come again, come again, come again?

Where have the seals gone? Where are the whales
That once used our waters before there were sails?
Where are the people who lived here before
And how is it, tell me, they're not here any more?

Brian Fitzgerald

No Answer

Once the seals had skins
shiny wet as a new anorak.

Now their skins have a rusty look
of an old car part.
The star has fallen out of their eye.

The seals have no answer
to the question
of poisonous waste.

O laughter
walk on water
that the seals may smile again.

John Agard

How Sad to Kill

How sad to kill
A seal or stoat
To make
A fancy ladies' coat.

John Kitching

From the End of the Pier

Held for a moment in the eye,
Bird-shapes
Rise on oiled waves,
Flutter into fragments,
Splinter into gold coins,
Dissolve into emerald shadow.
Treasure trove
Hoarded by the sea.

Catherine Benson

Puffins

The puffins' nests, deep underground,
Are egg-filled, noisy, full of sound.
The sea alive with food they need,
The puffins swim and dive and feed.

The oilslick, like a deadly hand.
The puffins, lying on the sand.
The puffins' nests, deep underground,
Are empty, silent, not a sound.

Ian Larmont

Fish

Look at them flit
Lickety-split
Wiggling
Swiggling
Swerving
Curving
Hurrying
Scurrying
Chasing
Racing
Whizzing
Whisking
Flying
Frisking
Tearing around
With a leap and a bound
But none of them making the tiniest

           tiniest

              tiniest

                tiniest

                  sound.

Mary Ann Hoberman

Riches

The ditch in Humber Lane
Was black with tadpoles, round
Black beads and whippy tails;
I knelt down at the side,
And filled my jar as black
As now I fill this page,
Glad of the gathered life
However many died.

Robin Skelton

The Fishing Trip

Little fishy in
the brook swimming
till he met
my hook !

Michael John Hodder (Age 10)

Where is the Frog?

Where is the frog
with his hop, hop, hop?

Jumping up the banking
from the bottom to the top.

Where is the frog
with his strong-legged kick?

Swimming without lessons
like a champion in the lake.

Where is the frog
with his shiny green back?

Sitting in a shower of rain
without a rainproof mac.

Where is the frog
with his sticky tongue?

Catching flies and eating them
all day long.

Where is the frog
with his glupp! glupp! gulp!

Happy living in the pond
for ever I hope.

Joan Poulson

Yoruba Poem

Enjoy the earth gently
Enjoy the earth gently
For if the earth is spoiled
It cannot be repaired
Enjoy the earth gently

Anon.

Enjoy the earth gently . . .

Take Care

In Spring
Green leaves
Burst bravely into life
Despite past dark and cold.

In six short months
They wither wearily
To falling brown and gold.

But Spring
And gentle rain
Will bring
The green again —

If we take care,
If we take care.

John Kitching

from Directions for Taking

Everyone should, all through life,
Hear the donkey bray
At the rising day,
Hurdy, gurdy, hurdy, gurdy,
Hear the donkey bray.

Everyone should, now and then,
See the peacock's tail
Spread a shivering sail,
Alleluia, alleluia,
See the peacock's tail.

Everyone must, lastly, lastly
Smell the empty air,
Outside, everywhere,
And nobody, nobody, nobody, nobody,
No body standing there.

Elma Mitchell

The Field

You might think the field is empty.
You might think no one's there,
but a million eyes are watching —
though you can't imagine where.

Under the toppling grasses
and half a metre in
the secret moles are working,
each with a velvet skin.

You can see their dusty castles
like sugar, brown and neat,
for a mole is good at digging
and he likes a lot to eat.

There must be a billion worms around,
beetles, and spiders, too,
and ladybirds and grasshoppers
and ants, and me and you . . .

So don't think the field is empty.
It's bursting to the brim.
You're treading on someone's larder —
mole, with his velvet skin.

Jean Kenward.

Stop!

Stop! don't swat the fly
Who wrings his hands,
Who wrings his feet.

Kobayashi Issa
Translated by Geoffrey Bownas and Anthony Thwaite

In the Garden

Out of the bird-bath, I
Lift up a shapeless struggling, and
See it on my finger-end
Change to a tiny fly.

What great things can be done
By love, and patient polishing,
with several legs, of face and wing —
Even a life re-won!

Roy Fuller

The World With Its Countries

(Can be sung to the tune of 'On Top of Old Smokey')

The world with its countries,
Mountains and seas,
People and creatures,
Flowers and trees,
The fish in the waters,
The birds in the air,
Are calling to ask us
All to take care.

These are our treasures,
A gift from above,
We should say thank you,
With a care that shows love
For the blue of the ocean,
The clearness of air,
The wonder of forests
And the valleys so fair.

The song of the skylark,
The warmth of the sun,
The rushing of clear streams
And new life begun
Are gifts we should cherish,
So join in the call
To strive to preserve them
For the future of all.

John Cotton

A River's Story

The fish disappeared from the river,
They turned up white bellies and died,
And drifted like dead men's fingers
In the slow-running tide.

They washed the river, strange as it sounds,
Till the tide flowed fresh and clean,
Then back came the fish, to flash and glitter
Where they'd always been.

Raymond Wilson

Save the Peat Bog

My Daddy saved a peat bog.
He saved it yesterday.
He brought home loads of farmyard muck
And stored it out the way.

'Six months behind the greenhouse,
It'll be as good as peat.
So, come the Spring,' my Daddy said,
'The plants will have a treat.'

Some people try to save the whale,
Or toads, or an osprey,
But my Daddy saved a peat bog.
He saved it yesterday.

Ian Larmont

We Must Protect the Countryside

We must protect the countryside —
the flowers and the trees.
We must protect the animals.
It's up to you and me.

Don't throw litter on the ground.
Please put it in a bin,
And close the gate behind you
To keep the cattle in.

Keep your dog upon a lead.
Make sure it doesn't stray.
Stay on the paths. Don't wander
Through the fields of wheat or hay.

Don't leave a broken bottle
Lying on the grass
Or it could start a fire
Like a magnifying glass.

Don't poke around in birds' nests
Or chase creatures that you see.
Don't pull up plants or flowers
Or break branches off a tree.

Don't squeeze through gaps in hedges.
Please use the stiles or gates.
Don't pollute the water
With rubbish or lead weights.

We must protect the animals,
the trees, the plants, the flowers.
We must protect the countryside.
Remember that it's ours.

John Foster

Recycling Song

(You all know the tune . . .)

What shall we do with our old glass bottles,
What shall we do with our old glass bottles,
What shall we do with our old glass bottles,
Early in the morning?

Bring them to the bottle bank, RECYCLE,
Bring them to the bottle bank, RECYCLE,
Bring them to the bottle bank, RECYCLE,
Early in the morning!

Where shall we take our carrot peelings,
Where shall we take our carrot peelings,
Where shall we take our carrot peelings,
Early in the morning?

Put them on the compost heap, RECYCLE,
Put them on the compost heap, RECYCLE,
Put them on the compost heap, RECYCLE,
Early in the morning!

What shall we do with our old newspapers,
What shall we do with our old newspapers,
What shall we do with our old newspapers,
Early in the morning?

Take them to the paper-bank, RECYCLE,
Take them to the paper-bank, RECYCLE,
Take them to the paper-bank, RECYCLE,
Early in the morning!

What shall we do with the litter-throwers,
What shall we do with the litter-throwers,
What shall we do with the litter-throwers,
Early in the morning?

Drop 'em on the compost heap, RECYCLE,
Drop 'em on the compost heap, RECYCLE,
Drop 'em on the compost heap, RECYCLE,
Early in the morning!

Judith Nicholls

This Land is Mine

The earth diggers came rolling
Across the farmer's land.
A huge sign-board was put up
'MINE — OPEN CAST' was planned.

My friend and I loved playing
In those green fields all day.
We ran home to our parents
To see what they would say.

Our families got together.
They wrote to Downing Street.
A man came up to see us,
He said we all should meet.

The open cast mine owner
Told us that we should know,
The fields would be re-landscaped
In fifteen years or so.

But we knew of a flower,
An orchid, very rare.
We told the man from London,
He said, 'Please take me there!'

We found the patch of flowers.
He cheered and said, 'That's it!
The land must be protected,
There'll be no black, coal pit.'

So we can play tomorrow,
The land is National Trust.
The grass is full of flowers,
And not the black, coal dust.

Wendy Larmont

Riddle

For want of a word
the thought was lost;
for want of a thought
the tree was lost;
for want of a tree
the forest was lost;
for want of the forest
a land was lost;
for want of a land
the people were lost;
and all for the want
of one small word . . .

why?

Judith Nicholls

Dawn Haiku

Dawn is born again
Gentle wind blows through damp grass
Let it stay that way

Colin White (Age 11)

Happy Thoughts

The world is so full
of a number of things,
I'm sure we should all
be as happy as kings.

Robert Louis Stevenson

The Fish in the Water

The fish in the water is silent,
the animal on the earth is noisy,
the bird in the air is singing.
But Man has in him
the silence of the sea,
the noise of the earth
and the music of the air.

Rabindranath Tagore

Let's Keep It

Let's keep it blue
The sky
The sea
Let's keep it green
The grass
The tree
Let's keep it clean
The sky
The sea
It's up to you
It's up to me
The grass
The tree
The sky
The sea
Let's keep it
Let's keep it.

Ian McMillan and Martyn Wiley

INDEX OF TITLES AND FIRST LINES

(Titles in italics)

ACKNOWLEDGEMENTS

The editor and publisher are grateful for permisssion to reproduce the following copyright poems in this anthology.

John Agard, 'No Answer', from *Laughter Is An Egg* (Penguin, 1990). Reprinted by kind permission of John Agard c/o Caroline Sheldon Literary Agency. **Matthew Baird**, 'All Things Bright'. Reprinted by permission of Walton C.E.V.C. Primary School. **Harry Behn**, 'Trees' from *The Little Hill*, © 1949 by Harry Behn, © renewed 1977 by Alice L. Behn. Reprinted by permission of Marian Reiner. **Catherine Benson**, 'Grasslands', 'Wild Flower', and 'From the End of the Pier', all © Catherine Benson 1993. Reprinted by permission of the author. **Gerard Benson**, 'The Elephant Dance', © 1993 Gerard Benson. Reprinted by permission of the author. 'The Bear' from *The Magnificent Callisto* (Blackie Ltd) , © Gerard Benson 1992. Reprinted by permission of the author and publisher. **Alan Bold**, 'Seeds', © 1993 Alan Bold. Reprinted by permission of the author. **Ann Bonner**, extract from 'Forest', © 1993 Ann Bonner. Reprinted by permission of the author. **Martin Cook**, 'Whale Haiku'. Reprinted by permission of Walton C.E.V.C. Primary School. **John Cotton**, 'Riddle (egg)' and 'The World With Its Countries', © 1993 John Cotton. Reprinted by permission of the author. **Richard Edwards**, 'Ten Tall Oaktrees' and 'Percy Pot-Shot', © the author. **Children of Elland Church of England Junior School**, 'Rhino on the Run', reprinted from *The Sounds Natural Songbook*. By permission of World-Wide Fund for Nature (UK). **Robert Fisher**, 'Fun fun fungi', © 1993 Robert Fisher. Reprinted by permission of the author. **Brian Fitzgerald**, 'Where Have the Seals Gone?', reprinted from *Alleluya!*, ed. David Gadsby and John Hoggarth. © the author. **John Foster**, 'We Must Protect the Countryside', © 1991 John Foster, first published in *Catching the Light*, ed. Brian Moses (WWF UK). Reprinted by permission of the author. **Mick Gowar**, 'Machine Riddle ' from *Third Time Lucky*, © Mick Gowar 1988. Published by Viking Kestrel and in Puffin Books. Reprinted by permission of the publisher and Murray Pollinger Ltd. **David Harmer**, 'My Future' and 'Our Tree', © 1993 David Harmer. Reprinted by permission of the author. **Mary Ann Hoberman**, 'Fish', from *Hello and Good-Bye* (Little Brown), © 1959, renewed 1987 by Mary Ann Hoberman. Reprinted by permission of Gina Maccoby Literary Agency. **Michael Hodder**, 'The Fishing Trip'. Reprinted by permission of St. Germans C of E Voluntary Aided Primary School. **Kobayashi Issa**, 'Stop! Don't swat the fly', from *The Penguin Book of Japanese Verse*, translated by Geoffrey Bownas and Anthony Thwaite (Penguin Books, 1964) , © Geoffrey Bownas and Anthony Thwaite, 1964. Reprinted by permission of Penguin Books Ltd. **X.J. Kennedy**, 'Hummingbird', from the *The Forgetful Wishing Well*, © 1985 by X.J. Kennedy. Reprinted by permission of Margaret K. McElderry Books, an imprint of Macmillan Publishing Company and Curtis Brown Ltd. **Jean Kenward**, 'Stones', 'Dandelion', 'Planting', and 'The Field', © 1993 Jean Kenward. Reprinted by permission of the author. **Sandra Kerr**, 'Do You Know the Fox', from *Birds and Beasts*. Reprinted by permission of A. & C. Black (Publishers) Ltd. **John Kitching**, 'How Sad to Kill' and 'Take Care', © 1993 John Kitching. Reprinted by permission of the author. **Ian Larmont**, 'General Winter', 'Puffins', and 'Save the Peat Bog', all © 1993 Ian Larmont. Reprinted by permission of the author. **Wendy Larmont**, 'Coal' and 'This Land is Mine', both © 1993 Wendy Larmont. Reprinted by permission of the author. **Ian McMillan & Martyn Wiley**, 'Everything's Got Its Place', 'From My Window', and 'Let's Keep It', © 1993 Ian McMillan and Martyn Wiley. Reprinted by permission of the authors. **Wes Magee**, 'Guard Wolf' and 'Humpback Whale', both © 1993 Wes Magee. Reprinted by permission of the author. **Robin Mellor**, 'Seal-song', © 1993 Robin Mellor. Reprinted by permission of the author. **Edna St. Vincent Millay**, 'Afternoon on a Hill', from *Collected Poems* (Harper & Row), © 1917, 1945 by Edna St. Vincent Millay. Reprinted by permission of Elizabeth Barnett, Literary Executor. **Elma Mitchell**, extract from 'Snail Appeal', © 1993 Elma Mitchell; extract from 'Directions for Taking', from *The Human Cage* (Harry Chambers/Peterloo Poets, 1979) and in *People Etcetera : Poems New and Selected* (Peterloo Poets, 1987). Reprinted by permission of the author. **John Mole**, 'Riddle - Snow-motion, lumbering . . .', from *Boo To A Goose* (1987) © John Mole. Reprinted by permission of Peterloo Poets. **Mervyn Morris**, 'They', from *Shadowboxing*, published by New Beacon Books Ltd., 1979. Used with permission. **Brian Moses**, 'Whale', © 1993 Brian Moses. Reprinted by permission of the author. **Judith Nicholls**, 'Riddle', 'Recycling Song', 'What is a Weed', 'Bamboozled!', 'Firelight', 'Would You . . .', 'The House that Jack Built', 'What on Earth?', and 'What is One?', all © 1993 Judith Nicholls. Reprinted by permission of the author. 'Wolf' and 'Whalesong' from *Dragonsfire*, © 1990 Judith Nicholls. Reprinted by permission of the author and Faber & Faber Ltd. **Grace Nichols**, 'I'm a Parrot', © 1984 Grace Nichols. Reprinted by permission of Curtis Brown Group Ltd, London. **Lydia Pender**, 'Giants' from *Morning Magpie* © Lydia Pender 1957. Reprinted by permission of Collins Angus & Robertson Publishers. **Joan Poulson**, 'Where is the Frog?', © 1993 Joan Poulson. Reprinted by permission of the author. **Rose Reeder**, 'I Know an Old Lady', © 1993 Rose Reeder. Reprinted by permission of the author. **James Reeves**, 'Words' and 'The Intruder', © James Reeves from *The Wandering Moon and Other Poems* (Puffin Books). Reprinted by permission of the James Reeves Estate. **Fred Sedgwick**, 'Christmas Eve', © 1993 Fred Sedgwick. Reprinted by permission of the author. **Robin Skelton**, 'Riches', from *Collected Shorter Poems 1947 - 1977*. Reprinted by permission of the author. **Ian Souter**, 'Surrounded by Noise', © 1993 Ian Souter. Reprinted by permission of the author. **Tewa Indian**. 'Song of the Sky Loom', from *Song of the Tewa* by Herbert J. Spinden, reprinted by permission of Grosset & Dunlap from *Out of the Earth I Sing*, ed. Richard Lewis, © 1968 by Richard Lewis. **Charles Thomson**, 'Acid Rain', 'Where Apple Trees Once Stood . . .', 'There's a Dragon', and 'I Spy on the Road', all © 1993 Charles Thomson. Reprinted by permission of the author. **Colin White**, 'Dawn Haiku'. Reprinted by permission of Walton C.E.V.C. Primary School. **Gina Wilson**, 'Red Alert', and 'The Weeper', from *Jim Jam Pyjamas*. Reprinted by permission of Murray Pollinger Ltd and Random Century Group Ltd on behalf of the author and Jonathan Cape Ltd, as publisher. **Raymond Wilson**, 'A River's Story', © 1993 Raymond Wilson. Reprinted by permission of the author. **Kit Wright**, 'Acorn Haiku', from *Cat Among the Pigeons*, © Kit Wright 1984, 1987; 'Song of the Whale', from *Hotdog and Other Poems* © Kit Wright 1981. Both published by Viking Kestrel and in Puffin Books. Used by permission.

Whilst every effort has been made to trace copyright holders prior to publication, in some instances this has not been possible. If notified, the publisher will correct any errors or omissions at the earliest opportunity.